Life Essence

Paran Mittal

BookLeaf Publishing

India | USA | UK

Presentation by *BookLeaf Publishing*

Web: www.bookleafpub.com

E-mail: info@bookleafpub.com

ISBN: 9789363317031

First edition 2024

Nostalgic Rain

This rain and this weather
Reminds me of moments spent together,
I really want to go back there forever
As now I don't see anything same as ever.

Rainy season and this rooftop
Where we played till the rain stopped,
Having no fear of what to do next
As we are always surrounded by our best.

The joy I felt in that rain of childhood
Still wanted to feel the same, I wish I could,
Stuck in this so-called free life
Where people are nudging each other to survive.

This rain brought a bucket of memories
Where I still live without any worries,
Hoping again for beautiful life ahead
Where a pinch of kindness and love for others
embeds.

माँ - निःस्वार्थ प्रेम

बिना जन्मे जो प्यार करे
और बिना देखे दुलार,
माँ तुम ही ऐसा कर सकती हो
दूजा नहीं है कोई उस पार।

बिना माँगे जो दे देती हो
अपना इतना सारा प्यार,
देख के मुझको ख़ुश होती हो
जैसे मिले हो मोती हज़ार।

और फिर तन-मन लगा के मुझमें
भूल जाती हो खुद को तुम,
कैसे क़र्ज़ उतारूँ तुम्हारा
जब रातों को सो भी नहीं पाती हो तुम।

बड़े होकर निकल गये हम अपनी अपनी मंज़िल
और रह गईं घर में अकेली तुम,
कहाँ से आती है इतनी शक्ति माँ
कैसे इतना खुद से संभलती हो तुम।

देखा अब ज़माना मैंने सारा
ना मिला तुम जैसा प्यार कहीं,
माँ तुमने इतना बिगाड़ा है
अब हर जनम में आऊँगी तुम्हारे साथ ही।

Healing Heart

In the middle of the night
When you feel this pain inside,
Your heart feels like ripping apart
Still, it will be alright.

Trying and trying when it does not get fine
And you keep changing your bed sides,
In the hope to comfort your heart
You breathe and exhale to refine.

All this chaos in your mind
Needs just a little more time,
When life's answers feel confined.
Take it step by step and soon you'll find.

In the middle of the night
When you feel this pain inside
Your heart feels like ripping apart
Still, it will be alright.

नमी

नमी है आँखों में तो नमी रहने दो
ना कहते हुए भी कुछ इनको तुम कहने दो,
ज़रूरी नहीं हर चीज़ बोलके बताई जाए
कुछ चीज़ें खुद से भी उनको समझने दो।

नमी है आँखों में तो नमी रहने दो
ना कहते हुए भी कुछ इनको तुम कहने दो।

सागर भी है कुछ ऐसा-सा
भर के पानी खुद में बहता-सा,
और क्या समाए है अपने अंदर, खुद उनको देखने दो
समझ के भी ना समझे कोई, तो फिर तुम बस रहने दो।

नमी है आँखों में तो नमी रहने दो
ना कहते हुए भी कुछ इनको तुम कहने दो।

ज़रूरी नहीं बारिश ही पेड़ों को तर करती है
कुछ बूँदे भी पत्तों पर असर करती है,
उसी बूँदो में तुम कश्ती को अपनी बहने दो
ज़िंदगी एक पहेली है, कुछ उलझी रहने दो।

नमी है आँखों में तो नमी रहने दो
ना कहते हुए भी कुछ इनको तुम कहने दो ।

Searching..

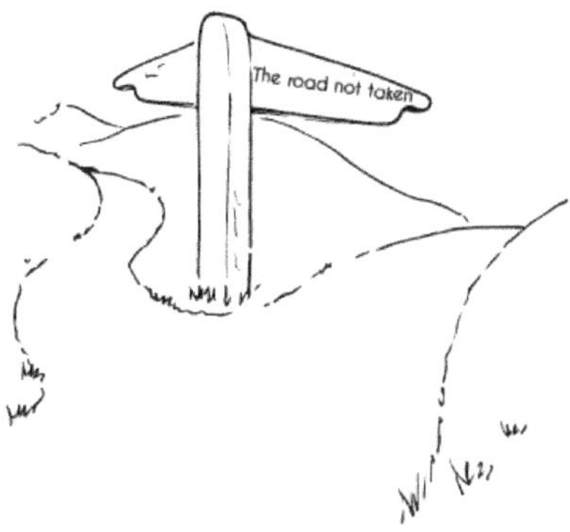

I am searching for the road
that will take me away,
to the less-suffering universe
to the more beautiful pathway.

I am searching for the world
where animals are loved than killed,
In the less competitive environment
where success is not mere loss and win.

I am searching for the nothingness
where you no more seek,
Satisfaction is not out there
but feeling of blissfulness within.

गृहिणी

मैं ना बोलती तो सुनता कौन
मैं ना जताती थोड़ा तो मानता कौन।

हाँ मैं सजती हूँ, सँवरती हूँ
घर में अपने झाड़ू पोछा भी करती हूँ,
अगर दूसरों को आईना ना दिखाती तो दिखाता कौन,
मैं ना थोड़ा जताती तो मानता कौन।

हाँ मैं आराम भी करती हूँ
क्यूँकि सुबह से शाम तक मैं काम भी करती हूँ,
अगर अपनी आपबीती मैं ना बताती तो बताता कौन,
मैं ना थोड़ा जताती तो मानता कौन।

मैं हर रिश्ते को जीती हूँ, निभाती हूँ,
प्यार और ममता से सबको सहेजती हूँ।
अगर अपनी भावनाएँ मैं ना जताती तो समझता
कौन,
मैं ना थोड़ा जताती तो मानता कौन।

मैं ना बोलती तो सुनता कौन
मैं ना जताती थोड़ा तो मानता कौन।

Midnight Walk

Night is exceptionally dark
But there seems to be some spark.
In the midnight silence
taking a walk in the park.

Unfolding the thoughts
The mind wants to embark,
Pulled by the breezy wind
Imagination got at the end of the arc.

Yes the night is extremely dark
turning towards my home,
Walking back from the park
carrying with me the moonlight spark.

WorthWhile

In the deeper space of your mind
where all your fears reside,
Just observe them closely
Think.. are they really worthwhile?

Each passing day is your reflection
Each minute you randomly think,
Each second is accountable to your life
Think..is wasting time really worthwhile?

Knowledge is wisdom you gained
Sharing it brings more light,
Be like your teachers and guides
Think..is hiding it worthwhile?

Get enlighten with your experiences
Get smarter with your flaws,
Be compassionate as you grow
Think. Will you be then worthwhile?

Pocketful Of Poems

Some poems are written at nights
and some when all is out of sight,
Some poems see the sunrise
and some linger all night.

Poems are written to inspire
and some to connect with their own lives,
In the middle of the chaos
you get some insight.

Somedays I write poem
Some days poem writes me,
It's a perfect blend
words keep flowing as the sea.

I would travel to nature's woods
to feel a little wholesome,
and returning serenely
with the pocketful of poems.

Aging & Balancing Life

You miss being completely free
Inside you many stories untold,
the heart doesn't want to agree
That's the gist of growing old.

From schooling to working life
Pat yourself for amazing strive,
Life is now a little controlled
But the child inside you
Should never get old.

We all say, time flies
Life happens in the middle of tides,
Who are you?
You are that same child
Finding yourself in this busy life.

This is the reminder
That you are enrolled into
 the chapter called Life,
Hold yourself tight on this rollercoaster ride.

अकेलापन

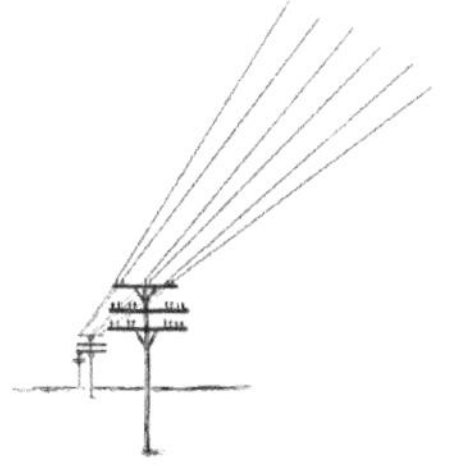

अकेलापन कहता है छुपके से,
अकेले हुए भी अरसा हुआ एक अरसे से।

खींच के ले जाती है एक डोर मुझे बचपन में
जहां मम्मी टिफ़िन पैक करती थी बस्तों में,
कहता है अकेलापन इतना अकेला भी नहीं हूँ मैं
याददाश याद रखवाने में बहुत पक्का हूँ मैं।

मेरे साथ बैठकर कर सकता है तू बातें चार
और हँस सकता है बचपन के क़िस्सों पे बार-बार,
ख़ुशी के आंसू भी तेरे मैं लेके आऊँगा
बस रहना कुछ वक्त मेरे साथ, सब याद दिलवाऊँगा।

भीड़ में खोके रह गये सब
एक दूसरे में ना कोई अब ढूँढे रब,
वक्त ना मिला ठहर के ये सोचने का
वक्त निकल गया वो माँ-बाप की आँखों के सामने
बैठने का।

अकेलापन कहता है छुपके से,
अकेले हुए भी अरसा हुआ एक अरसे से।

Realize

As I close my eyes, this picture in mind
Children on road are begging in line,
Mother struggling to get food for infant
And here we still complain about our lives.

As I close my eyes, this picture in mind
Where this old man has no one behind,
Hardly he can eat one meal a day
If we had the same meal twice, it's not our dine.

As I close my eyes, this picture in mind
Migrant labourers travelling by foot,
Hardly have basic ingredients to survive
But here we carry all anxiety, lying on a sofa aside

Lets now calm our greed and mind
We learnt enough during quarantine,
Show gratitude and rush less in life
Who knows the almighty is just by your side.

सीख

पहाड़ों की चलती हवा
कुछ बता रही थी,
जीवन बस साँसों का खेल है
ये किस्सा सुना रही थी।

राह में चलते पहाड़
और वो ऊँचाइयों का एहसास,
बता रहा था उनका दर्द
बारिश हो या धूप, छाया की उनको नहीं है आस।

और बहती नदी ने कहा
तू बस चलता जा विश्वास के साथ,
लगाव न रखना किसी से
खुद को ही देना होता है खुद का साथ।

जलती अग्नि ने समझाया
क्यों जलाना अपना खून को,
क्रोध, अहंकार और लोभ
मुझे में ही समर्पण करना है तुझ को।

To the Mind

To the mind…only multiplying the thoughts
Hault for a while and be still,
Stop judging your each thought
Untangle it, hopefully you will!!

To the mind…constantly processing
Take a break and meditate,
Just observe the thoughts passing by
You just have to be deliberate

To the mind…which holds memories
Distance it from your body for a while,
Try to feel this life as it is
As this journey is only valid till you are alive.

उम्र

मैंने देखा था रोज़ उसको ढलते हुए,
सूरज नहीं, मेरी उम्र थी वो,
अपने साथ जो जोड़े जा रही थी
अनगिनत किस्से
कहानी नहीं, मेरी ज़िंदगी थी वो।

मैंने देखा था उसको झुकते हुए
आँखें नहीं, मेरा अहंकार था वो,
जो दिखता तो नहीं था कहीं
पर आँसुओं में नज़र आता था वो।

फिर देखा मैंने उसको खिलते हुए
फूल नहीं, मेरा किरदार था वो,
जो अपनों की मुस्कान में महक रहा था
जीवन का अंतिम पड़ाव था वो।

Acceptance

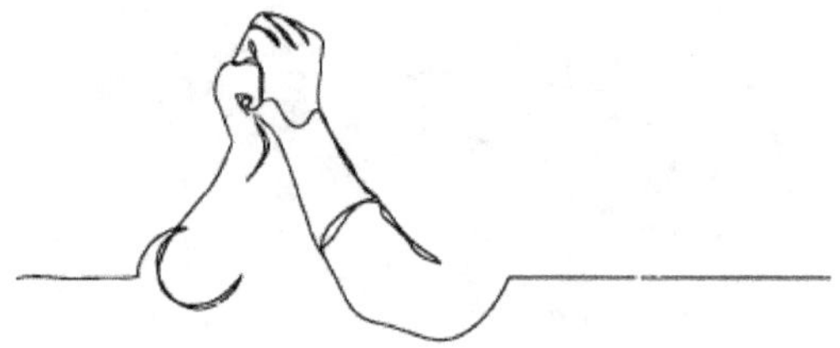

I asked myself, What is acceptance?
Is this something which will come with time?
or I have to first accept myself.

When I reach some conclusion
realise that it was a delusion,
trying to unlearn the repetitive pattern
and here my mind is in confusion.

In the middle of chaos, you lose your
independence
trying to change people and situations,
The part which remains unhealed is acceptance.

पतंग : एक डोर

पतंग कटी थी
उड़ के वो गिरी थी,
जानती थी फिर उड़ूँगी
दूसरे मांझे से ही सही।

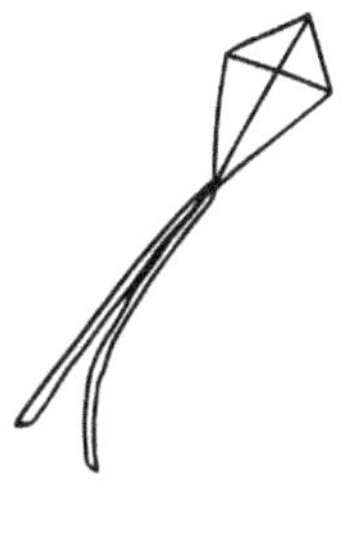

बिखर के जब गिरी थी
अपनों से ही लड़ी थी,
जानती थी घाव गहरा है
भरेगा किसी अपने से ही।

एक बदलाव जो हम नहीं चाहते
चला आता है,
एक घाव जो हम नहीं चाहते
भर वो भी जाता है।

पतंग कटी थी
उड़ के वो गिरी थी,
जानती थी फिर उड़ूँगी
दूसरे मांझे से ही सही।

Incomplete Love

Love always finds me to leave
to leave with another scar.
With another incomplete story
a chapter to close but yet too far.

Incomplete love is like a scar
which remains with you forever,
but it reveals that you tried
and keep us alive whatsoever.

In the end, it's about you
the person you became so far,
collecting yourself again
like the shining star.

उम्मीद

समझ सब आ रहा था
समय सब सिखा रहा था,
बस मन ही नहीं समझ पा रहा था।

अंदर तूफ़ान था तेज़ बहुत,
जो उस उम्मीद पे टिका जा रहा था।

क्यों ये वक्त रुक सा जा रहा था
कभी गुज़र जा रहा था हवा की तरह,
शायद देखने का नज़रिया है
मन की स्थिति की तरह।

एक दिन ख़त्म होने आ रहा था
एक रात रोशन होने वाली थी,
इस नोक-झोंक पे शाम जाने वाली थी
बस मन ही नहीं समझ पा रहा था,
जो उस उम्मीद पे टिका जा रहा था।

Silence - The Inner Voice

Does silence speak to you?
Or it makes you lost
Have you paid attention to it?
Or your mind just gets frost.

The ocean of thoughts
and rain of desires,
Oscillating between these two
Are you missing your inner fire?

Your heart knows the pain
the unspoken words inside,
In search of the true listener
where your heart can reside.

Moving On..

When all efforts come to rest
when all struggles find their nest
and the heart finds its strength
then the shadows of past quietly rest

The memories still come and go
of what was once dear
Now will gently fade
The path ahead becomes clear

Finding peace in the new journey
Where the heart smiles without any worry
Though the past was sweet and strong
The Future Calls—it's time to move on.

एक कप चाय

मैं और मेरी चाय अक्सर यह बात करते हैं,
प्याला भर ज़िंदगी और हम रूठने की बात करते हैं।

ज़िंदगी के कुछ अनुभव अनकहे,
वो कुछ आशाएं और उम्मीदें।
जो एक कप चाय पे बयाँ हो जाती हैं,
इतनी बात तो अपनों से भी नहीं हो पाती है।

फूँक मार कर फ़िक्र को उड़ाने का मज़ा,
सर्दी की रातों में चाय का कप पकड़ने का मज़ा।
शाम के जल्दी आ जाने का वक्त है,
एक कप चाय पीने का मन है।

चाय के साथ मेरा इश्क और गहरा हुआ,
जब-जब अकेलेपन ने मुझे छुआ।
ना रंग देखती है, ना पहचान देखती है,
खुद उबल कर दूसरों को स्वाद देती है।

मैं और मेरी चाय अक्सर यह बात करते हैं,
प्याला भर ज़िंदगी और हम रूठने की बात करते हैं।

www.ingramcontent.com/pod-product-compliance
Lightning Source LLC
La Vergne TN
LVHW041302200726
843507LV00014B/3097